MW00984791

Thorns of the blood rose.

the poetry of

Victor H. Anderson

edited and with an introduction by
Gwydion Pendderwen

Harpy Books
Portland, Oregon

Copyright © 2013 by Victoria Daniell
All rights reserved.

First edition, 1970.
Second edition, 1980.
Fourth printing, 2003.

Published by Harpy Books
an imprint of Acorn Guild Press
4207 SE Woodstock Blvd # 168
Portland, OR 97206-6267

All rights reserved. This book may not be repro-
duced, in whole or in part, in any form nor by
any means electronic or mechanical, including
photocopying, recording nor by any information
storage and retrieval system now known or hereaf-
ter invented, without written permission from the
publisher, except by a reviewer who may quote
brief passages not exceeding two hundred words
in a review.

Printed in USA

Thorns of the blood rose.

It is the cruelest month of all the year;
The frightened trees are frozen on the hill,
Their naked branches shaken by the breath of fear.

My senses quickened by the deadly chill,
I hear the silent moonquake in my heart
And in the virgin snow I read Her triple will.

Aloof in Heaven lonely and apart,
Among the peaks and craters of Her throne,
From out a nude black sky She flings Her silver dart.

Then like a stag I leap from tree to tree,
Running for shelter from the love I dread;
But true as fate, Her passion's bolt transfixes me!

Impaled upon the wood so lately dead,
I watch the boughs break forth in joyous green,
And from each drop of blood a rose of purest red.

On this appointed tree, most gracious Queen,
Your spotted Serpent sheds His gleaming sheath
And bows His head until the Star of life is seen.

From Earth, your fertile body far beneath,
Pregnant through winter nights and warm spring days,
The infant year shall rise to wear His kingly wreath.

Roses of blood and consecrated horns
Shall bless my head, and joy my cup shall fill:
But now for love of You I wear the crown of thorns.

Introduction

Victor Anderson was born in 1917, in the midst of the most violent conflict the world had ever known. While his physical entry into this plane came thousands of miles from the scene of battle, his spirit was affected by the war. He was born, he has said, in the wrong time and the wrong place, and in the wrong body.

It was evident to his parents and family that he was not to be an ordinary child. He was gifted, even in infancy, with powers that frightened and dismayed them, his clear, steel-blue eyes seeing through objects, his delicate fingers manipulating objects they did not touch. But at the age of two, he was struck by blindness, the powerful vision clouded by inoperable cataracts. Years of surgery and treatment only further limited the tiny fragment of sight left to him.

Despite his handicap, Victor was able to put his mind to work on studies such as chemistry, physics, literature and languages. He has a keen grasp of modern science, speaks several foreign languages (including Spanish, Greek and Hawaiian) and is a competent musician. His psychic training, obtained under the constant threat of punishment for consorting with Gypsies, Indians and other non-whites, brought the compensation of astral vision, telekinesis and other psychic powers befitting a shaman.

Victor's poetry reflects thirty years of struggle with a world that rarely rewarded his talents. Publication of the first edition of *Thorns of the blood rose* in 1970 brought him the public recognition he deserved, but it also brought him in contact with the Neopagan community, who were willing and eager to listen to his philosophy and learn how to use their own latent powers. Very few, however, actually made it as far as entering training with him, as his standards were both exacting and alien.

I have known the Andersons since 1959, so there was never a time in which I was unfamiliar with the alternate reality which formed the pattern of Victor's teachings. At about the same time that we published *Thorns*, we were engaged in developing the ritual material of the Faerie Tradition, and it was ever a challenge to wed Victor's metaphysics to traditional Faerie lore. Ultimately, we were able to put into writing a body of ritual materials adequate for an initiatory tradition of modern Witchcraft. The seeds of much of this tradition are the poems of this book.

The first edition of *Thorns of the blood rose* was sold out within six months of its release. Because the money for its publication came from Cora Anderson's savings, and the sales barely covered the expenses of publication, a second printing was not possible.

Gwydion Pendderwen

Part 1:   Many thorns.

Woman.

The kind of woman meant for you and me
Came never from the riven side of man,
But rose in splendor from the warm blue sea
On that grey morning when the world began.
Goddess of love and wisdom, fright and lust,
Knowing not good or evil, yet divine,
She knelt to clothe her glory in the dust
To form the living altar and the shrine
Between whose pillars man's first sacrifice
Was nightly poured to feed creation's flame,
Before the priests with fable's crude device
Sought to conceal the source from which we came.
So let us pray forgiveness and return
To our first temples, there to love and learn.

Widow at 3:30.

The night departing on swift silent wings
(Her lovely face turned to the western sky)
Has gathered up her dreams, and with a sigh
Takes one last look among life's broken things.
The new born day is near yet no bird sings,
The weary moon sinks down into the sea
Leaving the world to morning and to me,
While somewhere in the dark a church bell rings.
Unkissed and unfulfilled, at last I rise
And lay aside the tattered gown of sleep.
Why trouble Earth and Heaven with my needs?
I have a cloth of pride to dry my eyes:
The loveless world must never see me weep
Nor walk with grief in somber widow's weeds.

The silver grove.

I cannot promise love eternally:
Love finds her food and drink not in our vows.
Often we find the fruit upon her boughs
Vanished away in barren chastity.
Enraptured here we let our bodies sing,
Yearning to fill with love our mutual need.
O let no cruel law nor outworn creed
Untwine the arms or part the lips that cling.
Eternal faith I cannot swear, but still
Under the shadows of the silver grove:
Nine moon-white moments, and the triple will
Is satisfied, for we have offered love.
Come, while the moon along her regal way
Enchants the grove with pale ethereal day.

The shining hours of gold.

My darling, when some day our pathways part,
Do not forget me then nor lightly hold
Our silver dreams, the shining hours of gold
Wherein we held communion heart to heart.
Those moments like a myriad crystal spheres
Suspended in bright orbs of perfect song,
Atoms of time whose nuclei were tears
Unknown to science, hopeless to prolong.
Forgive the vows I made but could not keep
(So is it always when a poet loves);
I called your name the night I fell asleep
But when I woke there were no sacred groves.
Yet this frail aka thread that leads to you
Proves death a lie and love forever true.

My yellow rose.

In memory a fairy garden grows,
Each precious flower a kindly Negro face,
Arranged so every shade of color shows
Each little bud and leaflet in its place.
Tall, shapely blooms of regal black grow there,
Rich chocolates, red-browns, and ginger-golds,
A tiny copper orchid, darkly fair,
Smiles warmly while a yellow rose unfolds.
They grow more lovely through the passing years,
Too deeply rooted in my heart to die,
For some are watered daily by my tears:
I could not tell my yellow rose goodbye.
Some day in Heaven, if it be God's will,
I'll find her in my garden, blooming still.

Sonnet on an image.

Men would not call her beautiful, I know,
But misty moonlight crowns her lovely hair,
And on her lips and brow an Angel glow
For bright Apollo's kiss still lingers there.
Sweet Eros dreams between her noble breasts
Whereon my fevered head found more than peace:
Where I would be he folds his wings and rests
While grief is mine with tears that will not cease.
Now at the sweet remembrance of her voice
Such melodies within my soul arise;
Oh Love, how strange that I may yet rejoice
At having seen your shape in her deep eyes.
Give me the bitter cup, for it is mine,
Then shall I carve her image for this shrine.

Night sinister.

O night as dark and secret as my heart,
Whose core, a globe of incandescent blood
Suspended in an aching void apart,
Hangs like a dull-red moon above the flood
Of unshed tears, I watch the fading stars
Grow dim and lurid in the troubled skies;
Wild chords like gouts of flame from fierce guitars
Recall the tragic ardor of brown eyes.
Along the endless corridors of gloom
An opiate vapor brings enchanted sleep,
And opens to my inner eyes a tomb
For hope, wherein my soul lies down to weep.
All Hell and Heaven filled with your sweet scent,
And I had thought remorse and grief were spent.

The blind man to the harlot.

The blind man to the harlot made this will
When he unto his bed of death had come,
And all desire to live grew cold and still,
For low his heart beat like a funeral drum.
To you who reckoned not affliction's chains
As but a fence to bar my soul apart,
But soothed with love a multitude of pains,
I give my tears, my faded dying heart.
And may the Holy Ghost with purple fire
So purge your soul and body virgin new,
That in the springtime of a pure desire,
A better man than I shall cherish you.
And as escape from undeserved hell,
I leave the gentle Savior at the well.

Child of the Earth.

I walk this dark unhallowed ground
And from the vaulted womb of Earth
There rises with a grief profound
The child a mother killed at birth.

Drifting above the dreaming loam,
She wails with hunger and despair,
Crying for Mother, name and home,
Pale as sorrow, thin as air.

Upon my lips I taste her breath
Foul with the scent I dare not name,
And I am witness to the death
Conceived in craven fear and shame.

Why strive to touch this meager breast?
I cannot clothe your misty form
With flesh and blood to give you rest
And keep the spirit safe and warm.

I know the answer while I speak:
The love that brought you here to me
Falls from the Night-bird's cruel beak
Which bore my heart down to the sea.

Moon of all Heaven, clear and bright,
O Mother pure, O Goddess fair,
Spin from your silver wheel tonight
The curse that is a poet's prayer.

Recall the scene of brutish lust
(Passion perverted into greed)
And crucify the man unjust
Upon the cross of nine-fold need!

Dark of the moon.

We are so near and yet so far apart:
How strange that our two souls invisible
Should burn with such desire unspeakable;
O that some incantation of the art
Could move the Mother of all living things
To look on us with mercy in this hour,
To stay a while the casting of the flower,
And cut the bond from passion's prisoned wings!
With faith and hope I crossed the great abyss
Of empty nights and days to come to you,
Believing that our love could be fulfilled.
But now beneath your sacrificial kiss
My heart's blood mingles with that somber dew,
Wherein my fallen faith and hope lie killed.

The path of pain.

Dark is the path down which I walk alone,
Each step retracing every step we made
Love leads me on from shade to deeper shade
Of melancholy night where sad winds moan.
Recalling you, my heart is like a stone
Engraved with that dread prayer sweet Attis prayed,
Swooning in death while in the forest glade,
Crazed by his power, the great Boar claimed the throne.
As from the God's dear Blood, in time there grew
Roses and red anemones that tell
Love's oldest hurt to those who love in vain,
So from my dust in memory of you
O let wild blossoms breathe my last farewell,
Near to this path where I have walked with pain.

The fruit of lies.

I end at last my rosary of tears
On this dark bead above the cruel cross;
I've paid the coin of nights and days, of years,
Seeing always the vision of my loss.
Had you departed through the rainbow gate
Into the radiant world of Heaven's bliss,
And I had touched your hand an hour too late,
Your frozen lips beyond all need to kiss,
I would have wept and wailed in utter grief
Beating at Paradise with hateful cries,
But now with dumb acceptance and belief
I hold your parting gift, the fruit of lies,
That swells and ripens, fallen from the tree
With rotten sweetness and perfidity.

My night with you.

Loke, my night with you will ever be
A softly glowing pearl beyond all price,
An echo of that dear lost paradise
Where Love, the only law, made glad and free
The sons and daughters of the coral sea
Who sent their frail canoes out on the tide
With but a prayer, a star of hope to guide;
So was I drifting when you came to me
And steered my craft with tender loving hands
Toward the emerald atoll of your heart
Until the moonlit passage came in view.
And as we rested on the singing sands,
I gave no thought to when I must depart
The beauty and the grandeur that is you.

What subtle charm?

What is the subtle charm that will not set me free
When youth's red passion would another course pursue?
Does one seek blossoms where grey fungus spoils the tree?
A fragile violet pressed within a heavy book
Still clinging fondly to her passing hue
Would show the same sweet sorrow in her faded look.

Once in the dark of an old room I sat and played
Sweet melodies upon a rotting instrument,
And conjured up old thoughts not all my own, a shade
Still sadly phosphorescent with remembered light
Of yesterday's pale moons forever spent.
Now set, they will not rise again to fill the night.

Her hair is Spanish moss that to a ruin clings,
Her voice, a thin sweet echo of decaying pomp.
Like silver moon moths drifting on translucent wings,
Remembered joys still cluster round her tiny flame;
Like ghostly vapors flitting through the swamp,
They whisper still with awe her empty family name.

Late afternoon.
(To Leda.)

Little green-eyed madcap girl
In the yellow afternoon,
Your sweet elfin face smiling at me
In glowing gold, but under the moon
What will you be
When the stars careen and whorl
With your deep kiss?

You have shown me through your eyes
The great hymn the spectrum sings:
High violet and blue, the hum of red,
The dark brown flutter of wild lark wings.
The world was dead
Till you taught me to be wise
And walk with bliss.

Emerald-banded, orange-bright
In the black cloud of your hair,
Two serpents, their heads a double-jewel,
Writhe and coil in scented darkness where,
O sweetly cruel,
They consummate their delight.
What sign is this?

To Dimitrios.

When in the time of buds and green life springing
Beneath the whiteness of retreating snow,
I hear the birds of April sweetly singing
And feel the new-born sun upon me glow;
I bow my head in silence and remember
The fair, sweet youth I loved once long ago.

His father was of Kypros and his mother
Was from the isle where Sappho loved and sang.
More dear was he than sister, friend or brother;
As one we wept, as one our laughter rang.
Slow tears are falling now as I remember,
My heart transfixed on grief's dark bitter pang.

Here in the warm blue nights of summer weather,
Safe in the shelter of this fragrant pine
We lay and fashioned odes to chant together,
Then danced the round, his slender hands in mine.
As clear as any maiden's I remember
His sweet voice rose to hymn the powers divine.

The tree of Attis bears a fruit forbidden,
Yet bright Apollo and Hyakinthos knew
That long ago our love would not be hidden
But pledged with open hearts both pure and true.
Somewhere beyond all time the Gods remember
And judge me not because I weep for you.

My father.

My father was a blood-red rose that burned the air
And by his very presence blest the ones he loved;
He was an oak with mistletoe green in his hair,
Whom rushing flood or tempest never moved.

He was a joyous centaur stallion of the rocks
Whose form stood out against the copper sky of dawn,
Or he could be a Holy Satyr of the flocks;
Like Pan he loved, made music, and was gone.

I saw the red rose wither and the mighty oak
That kept us in his shade come crashing down too soon;
At that dread thunder something deep within me broke,
And where his boughs had been I saw the Moon.

Then filling all the seven Heavens with pure flame,
Arrayed in glory, walking barefoot on the sea,
Her body white as milk, a regal lady came
And bore his dreaming spirit far from me.

The temple of words.

Could we have met as pagan children meet,
Could we have loved as pagan children love,
Caressing Mother Earth with naked feet,
Raising our eyes and outspread hands above
To revel in the purity of blue,
I might have told with warm simplicity
The one, clear, shining truth of love to you,
Beyond the kiss, in rhythmic ecstasy.
But I must build a temple of my words
(Her many breasted statue of white stone)
While all my passions like a swarm of birds
Sing in the sunlight as I pray alone.
One word ill-placed and down the structure falls,
Crushing a broken dream between the walls.

Isabel.
(My first mortal muse.)

White Isabel, your memory remains
A seed of fire embedded in my soul.
Though passing years have dulled the searing pains,
I think of you when bells at midnight toll
And pine trees sway above the turgid flood,
While high in Heaven pale Hecate glows
Stark leper-white as if in need of blood
And cools her palsied fever in the snows.
When illness made your face more sharply sweet
You gave each line I wrote two quivering wings,
As beauty lay with horror to complete
The flesh along the hidden bone of things.
I dread the sight of you now that I find
The Muse departed, leaving dust behind.

Annalee.

Tonight the moon out on the meadow gleams
Through shifting veils of opalescent mist.
The fragrant woods are haunted by old dreams
Of little hands I held, warm lips I kissed.
O little Sister, precious in my sight,
Our joyous race to meet each golden day,
Your arms about me through the summer night
Were stolen secret hours of moonlit play.
Our love was half-again as old as time;
Perhaps bright angels knew such love to be
Forbidden here on earth yet so sublime
That when they took you from me, Annalee,
They left my soul, bound to the soul of you,
To mourn the sweetest love I ever knew.

The waltz I can never forget.

There's a song that lives on through the years
With a melody tender and sweet;
When I hear it my eyes fill with tears,
And my sad lonely heart skips a beat.
It reminds me of nights spent together
And a love still unmarred by regret;
Though I lost her one day,
She's still mine when they play
The waltz I can never forget.

When I used to waltz with Delores
All the world seemed so happy and gay,
There were numbers the band would play for us,
Other couples threw kisses our way.
Both our hearts were as light as a feather,
Drifting down from an angel above:
For when she danced with me
Everybody could see
That Delores and I were in love.

Blind beauty.

I stand amazed: how can such beauty be?
Can mortal flesh be molded to portray
The one true love in immortality,
The image of white Lilith cast in clay?
You are the word of love without desire,
A lovely shadow of the light divine,
An ornate altar without votive fire,
An empty crystal cup without the wine.
Your words to all your worshippers are sweet,
The balding, paunchy beast or foolish boy,
Their gifts are crushed alike beneath your feet,
You, who might quicken, live but to destroy.
So fate, the old impartial cruel and kind,
Has bid you, like the love you scorn, be blind.

To Madam X.

Since you and I have walked the world's dark ways
And spun the wheel of fortune at great cost,
Why then this wall between us? Must we gaze
On what is left to us and count it lost?
We talk of those strange heavens we have known,
Born of the flower that hides a scorpion sting,
Deep caverns over which our souls have flown
To watch that bright liquescent shimmering
Where things we dare not mention drool and gape,
Long twisted sins like writhing carnivores
From whose vile jaws the prey may not escape:
Their victims, pallid tramps and painted whores.
Yet from the very thought of love with me
You turn, a virgin sick with piety.

Laura.

Laura, I still remember how we met
Outside the tavern on that April night.
Voices were low, while phantoms of regret
Entered and vanished in the purple light,
Moving through shadows in the smoky room,
Each guided by the same slow pulsing star,
Now bright with hope, now shedding but more gloom
On those whose search for love has led too far.
White hands that clung to mine, a fair sweet face
Lovely and love-illumined as the moon,
A voice that called me back through time and space
Up from the lonely well, these all too soon
Rose like an angel singing, then were gone,
And I walked empty-hearted through the dawn.

Leda.

Don't pity me that I am partly blind,
Although my bitter soul cries out for light;
The Fates above me were not too unkind
For I have learned the wisdom of the night.
My darkened vision sees your elfin face
And in the lucid depths of clear green eyes
The wild sweet worship in the secret place
Where overhanging boughs obscure the skies.
Your lips descend to me, a glowing rose
That falls with crushing ardor on my own,
A darting flame between as they unclose,
Then all is dark save where we burn alone.
I breathe within the blackness of your hair
The incense and the passion of my prayer.

Just friends.

At last, Maria, you and I are friends.
What you have asked of me I give to you,
The golden cup of friendship full and true;
O tender hope of night, how soon it ends.
For you, the dawn, but in my heart descends
The waning moon cold in the sign of Ku,
While in your eyes the heavens' cloudless blue
Glows like a blessing as your sun ascends.
I saw two proud Ali'i pledge their love,
Their strong hands clasp above the altar stone,
A lord and lady of the land and sea.
But we, so like the falcon and the dove,
Must surely part; what is to be, will be,
I drink once more the bitter cup alone.

By Hellen's house.

We walked more slowly by your house today
Than we had planned to do. My heart and I
Decided not to pause but hurry by,
Till memory whispered softly, "Darling, stay.
See how the lilac flings her purple spray?
The dark red rose beyond my little gate
Is fully blown; last summer he was late.
The white ones didn't bloom till early May."
A stranger's light shines in the window now;
Another's footstep echoes on the walk.
She lights a cigarette beneath the bough
Of yellow blossoms where we came to talk
The night you held me for a last long while
And made me hide my sorrow with a smile.

A jewel for Cora.

Caught in this gem there is the purple hue
Of ancient sorrow, older than the earth,
Remembered from the night Kali gave birth
And stars came forth like rain when light was new.
I feel this holy mystery in you,
Love, dark yet radiant with the natal fire
Of primal dawn, the Mother's hot desire
Veiled in Her blackness till the God shone through.
Eternal passion, O celestial grief!
Youth and the tree immortal bloom somewhere,
Only the vessel breaks, but not the life.
Under the root the mold that was the leaf
Sheds forth the purple fragrance of my prayer
Offered in love for you, most honored wife.

Part 2: Awakening buds.

Song of Mari.

She comes at the first scent of morning,
As sweet as the breath of the sea;
Till the Cock of the Sun cries His warning,
She will walk in the garden with me.

Her kisses so wild yet so tender
Shall make of my body a flame;
No cloud shall obscure her bright splendor,
No veil and no garment of shame.

Though mortals deny and deride me
Till love must rise up and depart,
In a dread secret place She will hide me,
Sealed up with the blood of my heart.

For She is Our Lady of Twilight,
My comfort in life's darkest hour;
I see in the heavens of midnight
Her shield of omnipotent power.

She comes at the first hint of morning,
Her feet on the crests of the sea;
Till the Cock of the Sun cries his warning,
She will lie in the garden with me.

Secret meadow.

There is a meadow where I can go
And lie down in the cool green silence,
Where the sunlight heavy as white gold
Caresses the body of my mind,
The mind of my body.

Come all ye who are afraid of blood,
Feeling the hard enmity of stone,
Inhaling the incense you conceal.
Follow me with blossoms in your hands,
Your warm hands in white blossoms.

Slender young boys with hair like women,
Wearing the hyacinth of our sorrow,
Dancing with bare feet through the green rain,
Tenderly telling your beads of love,
Beads of love that tell of you.

Girls unchained in the meadow walking,
In nines and threes or in loving pairs,
You say no accusing words to me.
In the stillness I have lain with you,
And your stillness lies in me.

Let us laugh and play green marimbas
In the house built by desolation
And scatter our clear emerald notes
On the hard men with upturned faces,
The faces with upturned men.

There is a meadow where I can go
And find in the smell of burning leaves
The grass still green, as the healing light
Caresses the body of my mind,
The mind of my body.

Ceridwen.

I must obey Your quickening Triple Will
Though I may flee Your love with palsied dread;
At Your command my heart cannot be still
As I receive from You the holy bread.
When from the sky at dawn the moon has fled,
I keep the vision of Your moon-white brow,
Until the long awaited feast be spread
In Avalon beneath the silver bough.
Though You have bound me with no marriage vow,
My passion burns with this eternal need
That I may love You then as I do now
When from the broken clay my soul is freed.
No darkness can death's valley hold for me
If You, O Ceridwen, my moon will be.

Early moon.

Here in the still midsummer afternoon
The yellow sun clangs on the molten sea
While trees evoke a brooding mystery,
Caught in a moment of the vernal June.
Low in the east, O ghostly crescent Moon,
You watch the sun's decline indifferently;
Emaciated with what malady
Do you forsake the royal bed too soon?
Your brow is pale, your checks are flushed with green,
Chlorotic as a girl in her first flower;
A woman sick with unrequited love.
Yours be the ancient right divine, O Queen,
To drain my cup with wild insatiate power;
Descend on me and claim me from above.

Blessing.

You Whom all saints revile and sages name
Mother of harlots and iniquities,
For Whom the faithful bore the wrack and flame
Confessing vilest deeds and blasphemies:
By Earth, Your fertile body, blessed be,
And by the Living Waters of Your womb,
With Air, Your breath that moves upon the sea
And summons life green-springing from the tomb,
By Fire, Your spirit, blessed be with power
The children of Your love born unto wrath:
May light and cleansing in the unclean hour
Shine from Your moon-white brow upon their path,
Each unto each, eternal in love's way,
All blessed and illumined, Evo-He.

Among the hazel trees.

Come and drink of me
My beloved, my poet;
My waters are sweet and full of wisdom.
Come for inspiration to my deep well;
There will I fill your heart with understanding.
Walk among my holy hazel trees,
Under the shade of my apple trees.
Love has seduced her sister, Wisdom,
To lay with her naked among the willows
And feed on the hazel by my holy well.

Lift your heart to me,
Weaver of incantations,
The voice of the spotted serpent is sweet,
A bed of flowers awaits the young new year.
My fiercely burning star, my new born husband,
Place your lips to mine and drink of me,
Lay between my thighs and learn of me,
Know that man is for the woman made.
For I am life and death to life returning:
So you return at last to your beginning.

Witch love.

I find in you a love that seeks her own
Who reaches with red hunger through the night,
Still ardent when the body's strength has flown,
Regretful of a sheath so frail and light.
A long deep kiss, like to the charas thrill,
Your body arched beneath me like a bow,
A pagan soul that bends me to your will
By old forbidden rites our people know.
Dark love that burns with jealous tenderness,
No saint bewailing lost virginity,
But knowing well each intimate caress,
You hold me fast with selfish artistry.
A queen who holds her pride more dear than life,
You would defend your honor with the knife.

The witch's farewell.

The Mighty One approaches, yet I have no fear
Save only that which nature dignifies.
To cling to life is good, and honorable the tear
By which I bless the ruin that about me lies.
An awesome presence fills the room and lo,
The Mighty One is here!

There is a blood-red glory pulsing darkly bright
Where on His forehead gleams the jewel of power,
His great, black wings cast shadows where there is no light,
Yet in His hand He holds a lovely snow-white flower
Plucked where immortal golden apples grow,
In Mari's silver bower.

Farewell, dear friends and loved ones, I must take my leave
To wander through the Summerland a while,
Think not of me as dead when you have ceased to grieve;
I shall grow young again beneath Her radiant smile
That floods all Heaven with a moon-day glow,
Where age cannot defile.

Prayer for sexual purification.

Mari, most holy
Goddess-Mother of all living things
And Governess of the elements,
By whose Triple Will the planets move
And the clouds between the stars are gathered up,
Turning in stately revolutions
In the darkness of Your womb:

By reason of Your sweet love
All in heaven are made to rejoice.
Because of Your dreadful wailing cries
They that be in hell are kept at bay
And all souls in Your train of adoration
Walk on the wind to the high places
And whisper among the trees.

Whether You come as Nimue,
Slender maiden with the silver bow;
Or Mari, white moon who shines for all,
Illuminating the hearts of men;
Or Anna of the forbidden mysteries,
Whose black majesty, crowned with blue suns,
Reigns supreme in boundless night:

By Earth that is Your body,
By Water that is Your living womb,
By the Air that is Your vital breath,
And by Fire, Your bright quickening spirit,
I implore You to uphold me in my need,
Confessing now the impurity
Of my former intentions.

Help me to see the woman,
As in a sense Your incarnation,
And to see in myself the image
Of the bright God, Your Son and Lover,
To accept from wife or harlot the chalice,
Taking as from Your own hands the cup,
And to abstain without scorn.

Blessed be the Great Goddess,
Self-sustaining, self-creating one
Without beginning or end of days.
Through all things flow the milk of Your breasts,
Ever virgin because You are ever new,
Known of all, for You are all-knowing,
Eternal first love of man!

The price of sin.

Here I wander lost and lonely
On the sidewalks of the town,
With my deep bereavement only
Where the grass lies sere and brown.
Radiant Moon in regal glory,
Cleanse and cool my fevered soul;
Lady of the old, old story,
Sadly I have paid the toll
With nine silver pieces gleaming
To the hostess at the inn,
Paid the toll of hopeless dreaming
With the price of fruitless sin;
In the house of futile dreaming
I have paid the price of sin.

Till the sun shall rise tomorrow
And the world awake in day,
By the wan grey light of sorrow
Slowly I must find my way.
From my heart march long processions
Dimly seen through welling tears,
Martyred hopes and dead confessions
To the Mother of dead years.
Like a wound that bleeds forever
(Drop by drop each hour I live)
Comes the thought, Do mortals ever
Have the mercy to forgive?
Women love, but do they ever
Have the mercy to forgive?

Save me from the dreadful vision,
Patroness of all my pain;
Still the voices of derision,
Let my life be not in vain.
Lead me through the quiet garden
Bathed in healing crystal light,
Where the rose is red with pardon
And the lily spotless white.
Mid the fir-trees on the mountain
Let me weep where mourns the dove,
By the many breasted fountain,
Symbol of celestial love;
Many breasted silver fountain,
Shrine of your all-bounteous love.

Weeping willow.

Weeping willow,
Tree of Dolores
In love with the moon,
Bathing in her silver light
That tints your leaves with a somber hue
The color of sorrow:

In your cold feminine heart
You store up heavy water
Like unforgiving tears.
Yet the goodly virtue of your bark
Will cool the fevered brow.

Under these branches
The Dearly Beloved
(Sweet wound of my soul!)
Comes to me in holy dreams;
White as asphodel, Her deep-blue gaze
Bright with all-knowing wisdom.

Brooding willow tree,
Do you pay homage to the sun?
Or do you await
The forbidden caresses
Of the most ancient of Deities,
Enthralled by Her triple will?

Where the pure stream
Flows over black rocks,
I kneel in the clear grey light
And offer my devotion
To the womb of starry beginnings,
My first and last true love.

Midnight bell.

Toll forth in solemn measures grave as fate
Her presence to invoke, great bell sublime,
Eternal enigmatic voice of time;
Wake those forgotten dead who sleep too late.
Held in the wonder of this holy hour,
I see her walking on the moonlit air,
Tall, slender, ghostly white, with yellow hair,
Eyes blue as heaven, bright with triple power.
Mother and maiden whose virginity
At each new moon is new, though you are known
In beds alike of honor and of shame,
Bound to the wheel and blinded though I be,
Enamored of my pain to lie alone,
No hell could hold me should you call my name.

Nosferatu.

Last night I dreamed of you, my love,
And O! the horrid thing I dreamed
Insulted every star above
And each clear drop of dew that gleamed
On every hedge and tree.

Your body, precious to my sight,
Was swollen with obesity,
The form that filled me with delight
Was made a hateful mockery
In hell's revealing glow.

And she was there, the mistress who
On other nights did with me know
The ways of that dim world of blue,
Where broken men and women go
To drink the wine of tears.

She was so lovely, warm and young,
For hell had burned away the years
And given her a silver tongue
To sing with joy my hidden fears
And chide me for my sin.

Each well-remembered thing she said
Cut like a dagger deep within,
Till pride fell down and hope had fled
And I stood numbered with those men
Whose ruined souls lie bare.

You heard and saw but only sighed,
Your eyes grown dull and unaware,
For something dear in you had died;
And though I called, you did not care,
But slept an opium sleep.

My former mistress held me fast
With eyes that would not let me weep,
But made me watch the lives long past
Through which I vainly tried to keep
That poison moon-white flower.

I saw a man come walking by
With steps of slow satanic power;
At his command I heard her cry
As if it were the judgement hour,
"God has forsaken me!"

His whip lashed out and struck her face
Then twined about her endlessly,
Pulling her to the vile embrace
Of evil's ancient mystery,
The sore that cannot heal.

I called upon the Mother's name:
"Our Lady of the Starry Wheel,
The soul tormented by this flame
Wears on his heart Your holy seal."
And lo! the vision broke.

Safe in the shelter of our bed,
I heard the drowsy word you spoke
And felt your breast beneath my head,
As up from hell I gently woke,
And all the terrors fled.

In a druid wood.

Once in the stillness of a druid wood
Where ancient oaks retained primordial night,
Within a ring of phallic stones I stood
And heard the ravens calling in their flight.
Then from the altar table rude and grey
There rose a solemn word more sad than death,
And something lunar tinged the light of day,
A female power, a sighing chilly breath.
"Fir is to yew as silver is to lead,
My newly born sweet child and lover king,
O burden of my tears, my newly dead,
Crown of the oak and feather of the wing."
Thus spoke the holy presence in the gloom
Not with Her lips but from Her ageless womb.

The old Pictish priestess.

I heard an old woman say,
I have been a widow seven years.
My husband was killed while hunting deer
In the time of Mari the silent.
The last grey branch of an old dead tree
Fell upon him, crushing in his skull.
But when they told me, I did not weep,
For it was the holy time
Of the all-fruitful Bride and Mother
Whose sign is the full white moon.

Now I bless the young lovers
Who lie panting under the new moon.
Her horns have pricked them between the thighs,
Injecting their blood with warm honey
In the time of Nimue the Maiden.
I see in their rhythmic fulfillment
The path made clear for the soul's return,
For it is the holy time
When the Goddess pursues her lover
Whose sign is the morning star.

Now that I am growing old,
I shall not make a pale mockery
Of taking to myself a husband
With the vow to love him until death,
For it is appointed to me
To sit at council with the elders,
To gaze into the dark still waters,
In the aweful, holy time
Of Anna the Mother of wisdom,
Whose sign is the waning moon.

One night in winter.

My dearest, when I went in search of you
I found the wild beasts waiting in a ring,
Red tongues a-loll, lean bodies bunched to spring:
I dared not call your name, what could I do?
Their snarling turned the moonlight ghastly blue;
What were they tearing, O what piteous thing,
A scrap of fur, the feathers of a wing
Or mine own living flesh if I be true?
I had been traitor had I played the beast
And let them find your treasure near my heart,
Though in the primal joy of hate released
I could have rent their lusting forms apart!
Instead (O love forgive) I turned and fled
Far from the desecration of the dead.

Eros imprisoned.

I saw a thing that filled my soul with rage:
A bright-winged baby shape with frightened eyes,
Clutching the bars along his jeweled cage,
Praying for freedom with low fluting cries.
The men were bald, the women grey and old
Who viewed the tiny captive from the stars.
Inscribed in silver on the hand-wrought gold,
Their laws and creeds adorned his prison bars:
Damnations and decrees of "thou shalt not"
And hymns to glorify the gods of shame,
But never pity for their prisoner's lot,
Though he besought them in his mother's name,
Until she whispered on the wind and sea
The holy spell to set sweet Eros free.

To the Muse.

Eternal Mother of the Silver Wheel
Under the glory of Your milky way,
Night covers all as frogs and crickets pray
In holy convocation as I kneel.
Counting each hazel bead my lips entone
Enchanted runes and triple mysteries,
In praise of Your divine inconstancies
Lost in the aweful depths of love's unknown.
Our Lady of the sweet celestial pain,
Verr-Avna's wisdom to my songs impart,
Endow with quickening power till once again
Your oracle shall be the poet's heart.
O breathe upon the fires that dimly burn
Until for love of You the bards return.

Mari of the moon.

To Triple Mari of the moon we pray
And offer our devotions in the night,
For broken hearts who dare not dream by day
Shall find a refuge when Her healing light
Illuminates the city of our sins
And penetrates the soil with estrous heat
To burst the seeds where unborn life begins,
Releasing roots that grope with searching feet.
Unite the children of your love divine
(Eternal love the common herd calls lust)
From one another parted by design,
Scattered and blown about the world like dust.
Fate-driven, wronged and crucified in vain,
Deliver us, our Lady of the Pain.

The strange woman.

The strange woman,
    Night-walker on every street.
Above the city's hungry multitudes
I am the allure of the composite HER
Sought by every man but never found.

I am the cheap perfume in the dark hallway
Where the heavy steps of men clomp on the stairway,
Drawn to their fate by the scarlet thread.
I am there in the bitter mocking silence
After the last word that is always mine.

My incense floats above the altar
In the highest Cathedral.
My breath is the air over pine-covered mountains
Shining with fields of snow ever-virgin
Save for the sapphic kiss of the moon.

If you are lonely and would find me truly,
Go then by night to the hill above the city,
Lift up your face, adore and breathe me deeply,
Trusting in my fruitful orient womb
To bring forth morning and the Star of day.

I shall take as lover
The poet who sees in every God my Son,
And in the shape of every God his own
Dark shadow across the heavens magnified,
Burning on the southern cross for me.

I shall kiss away his blood
From the high altar of love's Cathedral,
Transfusing it back to him again
With the spring's first blossoms,
Giving unto him the right divine
To wear the brazen horns of the King of Glory!

I am the strange woman,
Night-walker in dreams you dare not tell.
Though profligate and saint alike revile me,
I am the black womb of every hope,
The final grave of every sorrow.

Quakoralina, the Star Goddess.

A lovely black woman is waiting, waiting,
In the boundless night.
A river of blackbirds are mating, mating,
In the dim starlight.

Down out of the sky they come winging, winging,
Drawn to Her black flame,
And the melody they are singing, singing,
Is Her holy name.

In the dust of Her feet are the hosts of heaven,
And Her star-sequined hair
Is crowned with a coven of six and seven
Blue suns burning there.

She has shown me the dreadful place of hiding
Where the Dove's egg lay,
The wonder and joy of the first dividing
Into night and day.

In love beyond love She is calling, calling,
Till the sea gives birth,
And the life-giving rain comes falling, falling,
On the fruitful earth.

Where under green willows a stream is flowing
There the tall dark pine
At his resinous heart is growing, growing,
With an urge divine.

Though fettered by chains in a world of sorrow
And the reek of men,
Her kiss has made me remember tomorrow
Where my soul has been.

The night will soon come when my spirit, flying
To freedom and rest,
Shall fall like a drone bee dying, dying,
Of love to Her breast.

Fugat spiritus meus tecum.
(May my spirit fly with thee.)

)ne summer night when all was still
A moonbeam lay across my bed;
Her look was pale, her touch was chill
As fingers of the living dead.

She kissed my brow and stroked my knees
Then placed her lips upon my own;
I felt my soul and body freeze
In holy terror trapped alone.

I watched my eyelids droop and close,
My heavy tongue too thick to speak;
As pure and white as virgin snows
I saw her hand approach my cheek.

She placed one hand beneath my neck;
Though fast asleep, I still could see
The other gently wave and beck
While from my fear she lifted me.

I floated free and light as air,
In radiant beauty quick with life,
To gaze with love upon the fair
Sweet Sister, Goddess, Mother-Wife.

More swift than light we sped away
To watch the world revolve beneath,
Blue-green and opal, bright with day,
Clad in Her misty bridal sheath.

The aweful sky was wide and black,
But not because there was no light;
It was a hue that summoned back
Most sacred memories of night.

She named the founts and wheels of fire
And all nine colors of the stars:
White Venus, planet of desire,
The orange-red warrior world of Mars.

She said: "Fear not this mighty gloom.
Seek heaven, but stay true to earth;
These are but ova in my womb
From which all Gods and men have birth.

"Through love you learned my secret name,
Because of love I shall not hide;
I am the darkness from whence came
The pure Bright Spirit, hot with pride."

She brought me back and, as before,
I felt the terror of the fall.
Into my narrow form once more:
My lips were sweet, my heart was gall!

In that strange hour before the dawn
We loved as mortal humans love,
But when I woke the moon was gone,
Leaving me only words to prove

That should I perish soon or late,
Hunger and thirst, or have my fill,
She sealed me with the kiss of fate
And worked in me her triple will.

Part 3:   Other roses.

The lesbian rose.

Dearest of friends and deadliest of loves,
Your red mouth blooms by night a poisoned flower;
In half-delirious dreams I wait the hour
When we shall mate like dark ill-fated doves.
Each knowing well the censure that awaits
The hidden love we dare not call by name,
We hide in terror while the hounds of shame
Bark in the street or whimper at the gates.
No pollen finds the bloom of our desire;
No place to rest, our hearts were made to break.
Thus are we cursed until the petals close:
Yet I will cling to you till I expire,
To love and cherish for its own sweet sake
The crimson beauty of this fruitless rose.

Talitha.

Warm within me trembles a secret longing,
But to hear you speak is to set it thrilling,
Singing through my blood with a silvery rapture,
Tender excitement.

Slender waisted, lithe as the growing willow,
Tilted breasts sweet as the fruit of heaven,
Snowy limbs so supplely soft and silken,
Stems of the iris.

I but see you walk and my body hungers,
Dry am I as dust with an empty thirsting
For one drop returned of the love I bear you,
Waiting in silence.

Dearest darling, only when I am with you
Does my life yield aught of its meager pleasure,
Light as air, enwrapped in a sweet forgetting
Born of your presence.

Would you flee in terror were I to whisper
Tender phrases born of my heart's deep longing?
Would you turn to bitterly scorn and judge me
Only for loving?

Sister, friend or lover in love's own image,
Yet I stand deprived of your love forever;
Still the fondest wish that my heart can offer
Ever is with you.

Now I know the meaning of Sappho's sorrow,
Why her songs go glittering down the ages
Though her hands and harp to the dust have crumbled,
Ever remembered.

When you have forgotten.

Paula, when you have quite forgotten me
Then shall I know the taste of what men fear,
Who hold no hope of immortality,
But watch the shadows lengthen year by year.
When you no longer say, "I knew her then,"
Or to yourself, "Her dreams were tall and brave,"
My heart shall know such grief as tongue and pen
Are helpless to express beside the grave.
If rain should lay the dust that once was me
And speeding photons summon life anew,
My love's warm red and blue-white ecstasy
Would paint wild flowers with memories of you.
Though you may cast me from you in regret,
Here or hereafter I cannot forget.

Ruth and Paula.

I wandered with male virgins in a wood,
A lonely mortal cast among the gods,
I heard their scriptures but half understood
Why only I could see the goldenrods.
Their ways, though kind, revealed a sense of wrong,
Soft Allelujas brushed my eager ears,
I joined the singing till another song
Of mourning doves fell on my heart like tears.
Then She appeared, an angel with dark hair;
Brown eyes, deep pools of somber mystery
That caught and held my gaze all during prayer
And with our souls we saw what had to be.
Can your strange heaven, far beyond the blue,
Hold such fulfillment as that night we knew?

Gay dance.

Pressed close together in the waltz we move,
Arms tight about each other in embrace,
Unconscious of all else as face to face,
Lost in each other, we at last find love.
A woman's golden laughter, warm and low,
Melts in the tender magic of a song,
You ask, How could a love so right be wrong?
Darling, I love you, that is all I know.
After the moon has vanished with the dawn,
Remembering these few moments we have shared,
Living again each kiss and warm caress,
I wonder if you'll laugh when I am gone,
Nameless into the well of loneliness,
Glad to be free of one who really cared?

Does Paula know?

Does Paula know I love her, would she care
Were she to feel the sweet oppressive pain
That thrills me when I touch her golden hair
Or think that we may never meet again?
Is she aware of all the many ways
Her image is rekindled in my heart,
As through the lonely nights and weary days
I feel her presence though we dwell apart?
What tender griefs, these memories of mine,
The farewell kiss, her fingers on my cheek;
Can love forbidden still be love divine?
Our hearts could answer if they dared to speak.
Whose law can judge, whose word can curse or blame?
I should not love her, yet I feel no shame.

Sisters of twilight.

Dear tragic loves, ill fated for whose sake
A double flower upon the altar glows:
Rose, red with ardor blooming in a rose,
Kissed by the blood of hearts foredoomed to break.
Strange how our paths lead ever side by side
In writhing patterns of some fell design,
Sin-shadowed, somber with a light divine,
To wells of loneliness where tears abide.
Elusive, unattainable is joy,
Run where we will or plead with outstretched arms,
Heedless of what vile word that warns of doom.
O twisted love whose hunger can destroy
Or wake with terror as the serpent charms
Dead hopes that find in each wild breast a tomb.

Träumestrasse.
(Street of dreams.)

Darling, when you are with me and we walk
The street of our forbidden love alone,
There are no words, we have no need of talk,
The sun has set, the rose is fully blown.
We pass by shadows, and low voices tell
Of bitter hope that dwells in hopeless state
Where love has built a paradise in hell
And sinks her roots below the tree of fate.
Each sees in each what others cannot see,
All they have taken from me you return,
While in communion with love's mystery
We bless the fire wherein our bodies burn.
These hopes and joys that live where daylight gleams
Are but confessions on the street of dreams.

I know.

I know you love me, dear, don't try to speak
(Kiss me and let my lips to yours unfold)
Nor count the truth of love less fully told
Or clarified than when against my cheek,
Wet with our mingled tears so soon to cease,
You murmured soft endearments strangely sweet;
Our bodies merged, my feet upon your feet:
Unthinking tender moans of wild release.
Love gives me wisdom to trace out the seam
Of bitter pride deep woven through your heart,
Vivid as veins of scarlet on green leaves.
Each time we love or lie awake and dream
My senses tremble to the alien part
Enclosed within your soul that always grieves.

When I loved you.

I loved a love wherewith all things are loved;
Sweet sister of my soul, when I loved you
I found the joys of earth and heaven proved
And all the bardic lore of love come true.
My hymns of praise winged to the highest star
And echoed through the caverns far below,
Till on the street where wasted women are
A lunar brightness made the shadows glow.
I grieved the grief wherein all things travail
As joy and sorrow wed to form the whole;
White Ishtar's holy lamp shone silvery pale,
But with the rain Her tears fell on my soul.
So stands the lover, sentenced and undone,
To see the one in two, the two in one.

Neon lane.

Red rules this portion of the street of dreams,
On every walk and window pane he runs,
Swift changing patterns of electric suns;
Even the shadows shimmer in his beams.
A scarlet centaur draws a flaming sword,
Night-blooming roses burn above this sign,
Dark words in Grecian letters tell of wine:
"Sweet blood of grapes by holy Bacchus poured."
Clad like a Roman courtesan in red,
All up and down three blocks on either side,
Radiant with gay abandon lies my street.
Light fills my eyes and whorls about my head,
Effulgent with a lustful ruby tide,
Tingling between my thighs with prickly heat.

Part 4:   Petals in my lei.

A tropic word.

Why must *aloha* be a tropic word
That withers in the smoke of northern towns,
When woodland songs, the sweetest ever heard,
Are born in breasts of quiet, temperate browns?
Why does *mahalo* (thank you) lose its grace
And music in the clamor of the street;
Should words like these transcend all time and place
Or hide in shame wherever strangers meet?
For all our many doctrines, ways and creeds
That seek a distant heaven as their goal,
We cannot deal with honest human needs;
With minds yet dark, how can we light the soul?
Where women really love and men forgive,
There may *aloha* and *mahalo* live.

When Loke walks.

When Loke walks, a noble grandeur floats,
As when an island of the morning sea
Lifts suddenly her forest covered crown,
And spreading rainbows veil in mystery
An emerald valley or an ivory town
Where fleets of little boats
Lie safe within the reef about her shore
In quiet waters bluer than the skies,
Where every ripple holds a glad surprise.
The time is near when we shall see no more

Such natural grace and simple dignity!
In her dear presence gleams a kindly light,
The golden splendor of our yesterdays
Before we said *aloha* and goodnight
To older, wiser faiths and gentler ways;
And when she speaks to me,
Holding my face between her lovely hands
To place upon my lips the longed for kiss,
My soul and being overflow with bliss,
And I remember, Loke understands.

Was it in a dream?

Was it in a dream
I reached out my hands to you
And our fingers touched?
I ran on the sea combers
For I was spirit;
Light with love of you I sped
To where you waited.
We laughed and the ocean laughed,
And the old, strong Gods
Whispered to one another
In the high places,
Kane and Hina, Laka,
Pele of the fire,
And the tall blue God who walks
The sea at evening.
I overheard them talking:
"They are our children,
We love them and wanted them
To be together."
But the dark clouds descended
With crashing thunder,
Tearing your soul from my soul;
And the strong Gods were weeping.

Your lei of sonnets.

For you a lei of fourteen-petaled flowers
I weave, but please don't ask me to explain
Why some are fresh with dew of forest bowers,
While others glisten with the dew of pain.
A deeper sorrow and a higher prayer
I count among the lessons I have learned;
That love has clear brown eyes and midnight hair
Is truth by which my heart is blessed and burned.
From *awapuhi* by a mountain pool,
Wild red *lehua*, bright as passion's noon,
Grey tropic moonlight, fragile, clear and cool,
And blood-orange sunlight on a bronze lagoon,
I weave with burning bloom and tender leaf
Your lei of boundless love and bitter grief.

A nymph of Maui.

Out on the cool lanai in my chair
I watch the sun sink in the western sky,
The lilac heavy in the golden air
Where glides the yellow tropic butterfly.
All through the amber twilight I can hear
The sound of tiny footfalls on the tile,
And lilting, silvery laughter sweet and clear
That makes the jasmine blossoms nod and smile.
A slender body rests in my embrace
As soft brown arms about my neck are thrown,
And firm, sweet kisses on my lips and face
Make me forget I ever lived alone.
Lehua o ka lani from above,
My nymph of Maui, made for life and love.

Love looks at the clock.

What are these seconds,
Atoms of time measured out
By our own decree?
I ask the Mother of time,
"What is my meaning?"
Great universal ocean!
How thin and fragile
Is this unworthy vessel
Holding this portion
Of your water that is "I"
In the lotus cup
Two clear drops fall together,
Shining in its heart
With subtle, changing colors.
In the bright morning,
Twin drops in love with the light
Rise in the white mist
And become one cloud of love
In perfect union.
Mother love, father wisdom,
By one silver thread
Bound to the waters below
In the soft petals.
O the night of becoming,
O the day of fulfillment!

Those were Hawaiian nights.

Those were Hawaiian nights I spent with you,
Though in the city streets cold northern rain
Came dressed in fog to tap the window pane.
In our apartment skies were starry blue,
We kissed, and lo! a great Hawaiian moon
Leaped ghostly white above the sighing sea.
You drew me near and gave your all to me
While heaven burned and vanished all too soon.
And when the moon had set, you held me still,
Your understanding smile and wan caress
Sought vainly to retain the cherished thrill,
To shield from dawn our shattered happiness.
Then on a cold grey morning without tears,
We said goodbye and faced the lonely years.

The blue shell.

Darling, don't ask me now, I cannot tell
The reason why I tossed your gift away,
That tiny blue pagoda of a shell
Back to the curling comber's hissing spray.
The moment when it touched my outspread hand
I felt the mana flow, my arm grew cold,
As light congealed out on the rippled sand
Into a form of clear etheric gold.
She saw my spirit through deep violet eyes,
My heart beat to the drum of other days;
Bright emerald hair down to her glowing thighs
Was beauty worthy highest hymns of praise.
All through the night as you lay close to me,
I yearned toward the melancholy sea.

If I grow weary.

If I grow weary of the singing sea,
No longer thirsting for the greens and blues
Between the foaming crests at Waikiki,
Nor thrill with rapture to the sunset hues,
I've lived too long; so lay me in the sod
That I may nourish slender stalks of cane,
And when the tradewinds blow my soul to God
I will remember and drift back again.
For all the love, dark bitterness and joy
That in Hawaii's proud high bosom burns,
The chilling hand of death cannot destroy
Or still the aching heart that grieves and yearns.
I will return to keep the tryst divine,
For I am hers and she forever mine.

House of sighs.

Why do I haunt this old, grey house of sighs
And spin with spiders here my dusty dreams,
Where fitful wind in bitter sadness cries
On dry grey rot that molders in the beams?
These rooms once felt the tread of dancing feet,
And though to other ears those songs are mute,
They will return to me as dear and sweet
As melodies played on a ghostly flute.
A fairy step, a phosphorescent face
And love has pierced the silvery veil between,
Illumined by a soft immortal grace,
Each well-remembered form is briefly seen.
This old, grey house is mine to have and hold
Though joy is theirs and glories yet untold.

Part 5: The thorn cuts deep.

Hospital.

I hear low whispers at the narrow bed
Where lies a milk-white youth in bitter pain.
I hear a mother weeping for the dead,
The still-born dead: Gethsemane in vain.
In these white wards it is the midnight hour,
My mouth is dry, I too await the knife
Where evil comes up like a silent flower
And terror wakes to cold, putrescent life.
Do you who wander out in God's sweet air
Ere think that you into this place may fall,
To scream the scream that is beyond a prayer
Or hear them wheel the horror down the hall?
My God, the things these whited walls could tell
Of mystic ether-sleep and waking hell.

The prostitute.

When I behold the evil in men's eyes
And read the vile predictions of my fate,
Hearing the life-watch tick "too late, too late,"
My soul recoils in horror and surprise.
Then from my flesh I feel the Goddess rise,
Her bloody menstrual moon dark red with hate!
And I envision cities desolate,
Where broken dreams are garbage, green with flies;
Their restless maggots seethe, pale leprous worms
Who cannot die beneath the flaming sun
Nor with his hellish ardor come to terms,
But writhe and palpitate till it is done;
They will not cease, however deep the night,
To feed until my very bones are white.

The bum.

I have not always roamed the world like this,
A filthy, drunken bum out in the street;
These bearded, weathered lips knew how to kiss
Before they learned to curse and beg for meat.
I walk in rotten rags and dirty feet
Where hunger burns, a self consuming flame.
Mine is the story useless to repeat;
When pride and hope are gone, who needs a name?
Somewhere along the road that leads to shame,
I lost the thing you preachers call my soul.
I can't remember now who was to blame,
It's been so long since I was clean and whole.
So call me Bum and let the world despise
Their own begotten vomit and look wise.

Saint Laverna.

I met her in a narrow alleyway
Between an old slum mission and a bar,
A slender waif in worn blue jeans, a stray
Whose cigarette, a warm red pulsing star,
Revealed a face fear-haunted, with such eyes
As need no ray, however dim the spark,
To gaze in pity but without surprise
On deeds of rape and murder in the dark.
Her hair was rumpled and her ferret smell
Enflamed my passion with its wild perfume,
And in a place whose name I dare not tell
I lay with Sorrow in a lightless room;
Where, at the moment of our ecstasy
I moaned, "Oh Saint Laverna, pray for me!"

A question to the dust.

I would ask a question of the dust,
The grey dust of travel,
The brown road dust:
Where are the gypsies?
Only last night I was with them,
My ears still ring with their laughter
Still vibrating to the singing strings
Of trilling mandolins
That cry farewell,
Leaving me bereft.

Where is the wise old mother whose eyes
Kindled my wild spirit,
Burning old bonds
And inhibitions?
She knew the true nature of dreams,
Sleep was to her but a gateway
Through which her soul, spinning a grey thread
From between her dark eyes,
Trod the blue air
To the near country.

By the hissing campfire's orange gold
I watched Karmelita,
Lean, barefooted,
Her throaty voice harsh
In high breathless songs of passion,
Her legs tawny serpents of love,
Thighs and hips writhing in red hunger.
Like little sharp-billed birds,
Her round, young breasts
Strove to fly to me.

Only yesterday the old man said,
"We are bent easily,
But we don't break."
And I remembered
As from a former life the day
The children of the sun took flight,
Swarming bees laden with rich booty,
Pilfered as on they flew
From friend and foe
And the gadzi hoard.

I would ask a question of the smoke
Blown over the railroad,
The campfire smoke:
Where are my gypsies?
Where is old Mother Lorita?
And the weathered violinist?
Where is love-hungry Karmelita?
A question to the dust,
To the grey smoke
And the cool, blue wind.

Insomnia.

There is a mill that grinds and grinds,
There is a book with lines and lines,
There is a spring that winds and winds,
But never breaks.
There is a car with wheels and wheels,
There is a thief who steals and steals,
There is a heart that feels and feels,
But never aches.

God, stop the mill that grinds and grinds,
God, close the book with lines and lines,
Release the spring that winds and winds,
Don't let it break.
God, stop the car with wheels and wheels,
God, curse the thief who steals and steals,
But change the heart that feels and feels,
O let it ache.

Los olvidados.
(The forgotten ones.)

I walk by the graves in the morning
While the last light of dawn is still grey,
And a dove on her nest coos a warning
Of the terror that wanders by day.

I have looked on the marbles of loved ones
And recalled the dear voices of yore,
Now with reverence I think of the lost ones
And the names that are spoken no more.

At night when the cool rain is falling
And the hours before daylight seem long,
From the dark womb of earth they are calling
As she murmurs an old cradle song

To erase the old sins unforgiven,
To release from their hatred and lust
All the souls who are searching for heaven
And the bodies that crumble to dust.

But how can a poet remember
Foreign lips that no longer have breath,
And from ashes too old for an ember
Summon that which was taken by death?

En el nombre de los olvidados
Whether buried on land or at sea,
Los Santos y pobres bravados
Who have prayed, sinned and suffered like me,

I invoke the Black Angel's dread powers,
With the heart beating slow in my breast,
In the name of our Lady of Flowers
And the loves that may never have rest,

Till my soul, like a ship proudly sailing
Where the light flickers lurid and red,
Journeys far through the laughter and wailing
To return with the words of the dead.

Miscellany: Humorous Pieces

The morlywort.

The morlywort's an ongful gritch
The parson wouldn't care to know,
Its house is circled by a ditch
Where yarp-infested ichors flow.

Their world is lit by two hot suns
One calcious white, one moony blue,
So while they munch lysergic buns
The morlys dream the white day through.

But when the deep-blue sun is high,
This androgynous vege-table
Will drink the Rumdum river dry
Then vorr as long as it can rable.

No moral has the morlywort
To warp its lasbracivious mind;
No Ten Commandments spoil the sport
By which it propagates its kind.

In Bombo's temple three by three
(That's how the morlyworts are married)
They workel 'neath the shlopskush tree
Where once langsyne the gutch was harried.

There while the red-green sap gersplats
The gollywhomptious Gods of good
Will bless them as they eat their hats,
Before the Juju made of wood.

For ritual is the boogaloo
The morlyworts all dig the most,
"Thou shall not marry two by two"
Thus sayeth our Father-Mother's ghost.

If you would enter Morlyland,
Become you like the human child,
With slurpy tongue and sticky hand
Blood-loving, hip and crazy-wild.

If earthmen ever find a way
To travel to the distant stars,
We morlyworts will zap your shay
With kapu thorns and huhu bars!

Before election.

In the days before election
When politics has B. O.
And the ardor of our affection
For our fellow man burns low,
In the fervor of Christianity
Or the artistry of profanity,
Sing the glory of your vanity
All ye who are free,
You, too, John Doe.

Traveling girl.

Jenny brought back little Jane
From a recent trip to Spain,
Then she brought back Jack and Jill
On returning from Brazil.

Donna, Marie, Suzette and Vance
Were souvenirs of sunny France,
Till Papa cried in tones perplexed,
"Oh Jenny, are you over-sexed?"

Disappointment.

I took Miss Twye down by the river
Where the reeds and cat-tails quiver.
There I made a nest of grass
For my dainty slender lass.
Before I got what I was wishing,
Some darned fool came that way fishing.